DADS
by
Howie Rubin

Illustrated by Doug Hastings

HOWIE HAUS BOOKS Portland, OR

Printed in Singapore
1   2   3   4   5   6   7   8   9   10
Publisher's Cataloging-in-Publication
(Provided by Quality Books, Inc.)

Rubin, Howie
        Dads / by Howie Rubin ; Illustrated by Doug Hastings.
– 1st ed.
        p. cm.
        SUMMARY: This multicultural look at what being a dad
is really all about in the contemporary world.
        Audience: Ages 5-13
        LCCN 00-193062
        ISBN 0-9703971-1-9

        1. Father and child – Juvenile literature. 2. Fathers
– Juvenile literature. I. Title

        HQ755.85.R83 2001   306.874'2
                                                QB100-901836

This book is dedicated to

Irving Rubin

1914-1995

Any man can be a father,
but it takes a *great* man to be a Dad.

What makes a Dad
so special?

When I'm hungry,

Dad feeds me.

When I'm wet,

Dad makes sure
I have a
dry diaper.

When I take my first steps,

Dad waits with open,
loving arms to catch me.

Dad shows me how
to brush my teeth

and comb my hair.

Dad takes me for walks.

We talk
about our day...

and discover
new things
together.

Dad shares his favorite

childhood games with me.

When I'm sad
or hurt,
Dad
comforts me.

After meals, Dad shows me how to wash the dishes.

Dad teaches me how to play
his favorite sports.

When I need help with my homework,

Dad helps me

find the answer.

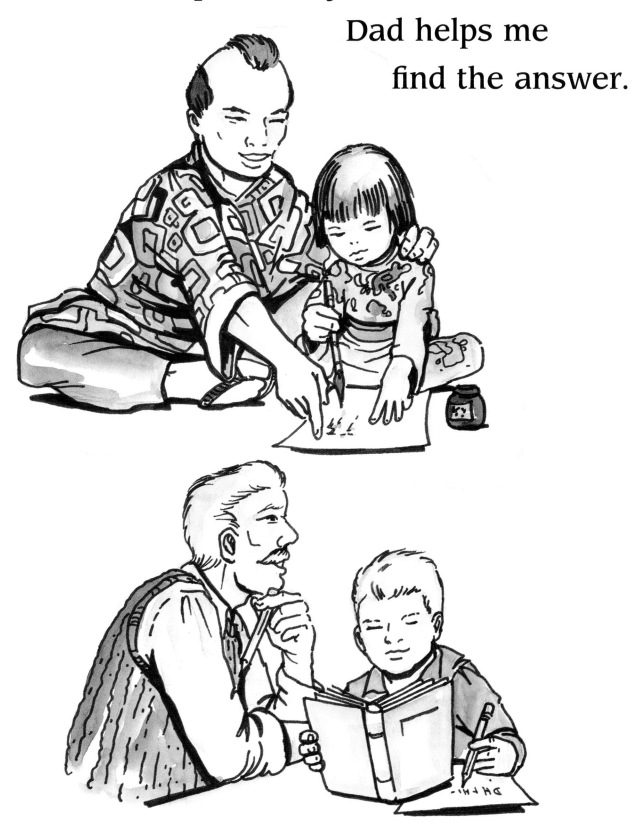

Before I go to sleep at night,
Dad reads
me a story.

Dad teaches me how to do the household chores.

When I'm old enough, Dad teaches me how to cook my own meals.

Dad teaches me to ride a horse...

and drive a car.

Some kids have Dads that teach them how to drive tractors!

Dad teaches me to mow the lawn

and produce food
from the earth.

I get to teach Dad new things too,
like how to use a computer.

Dads teach us to realize our potential,

follow our dreams,

and help us be the best human being.

Dads guide us through life
and point us in the right direction.

Best of all,

Dads love us very much.

PLACE YOUR
DAD'S PICTURE
HERE

My Dad